Poems about F

Selected by Brian M

GW01459903

Contents

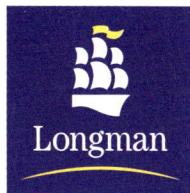

Longman

Edinburgh Gate
Harlow, Essex

Skipping Song

Jump down low,
    jump up high.
Stretch up tall
    and touch the sky!

Jump up high,
    jump down low.
Touch the rope
    and out you go!

Moira Andrew

At the Playground

When we went to
    the playground
I swung on the swings,
I slid on the slide,
I hung from the rings.
I raced over to Mum
for a kiss and a cuddle,
but as we were leaving,
I fell in a puddle!

Brian Moses

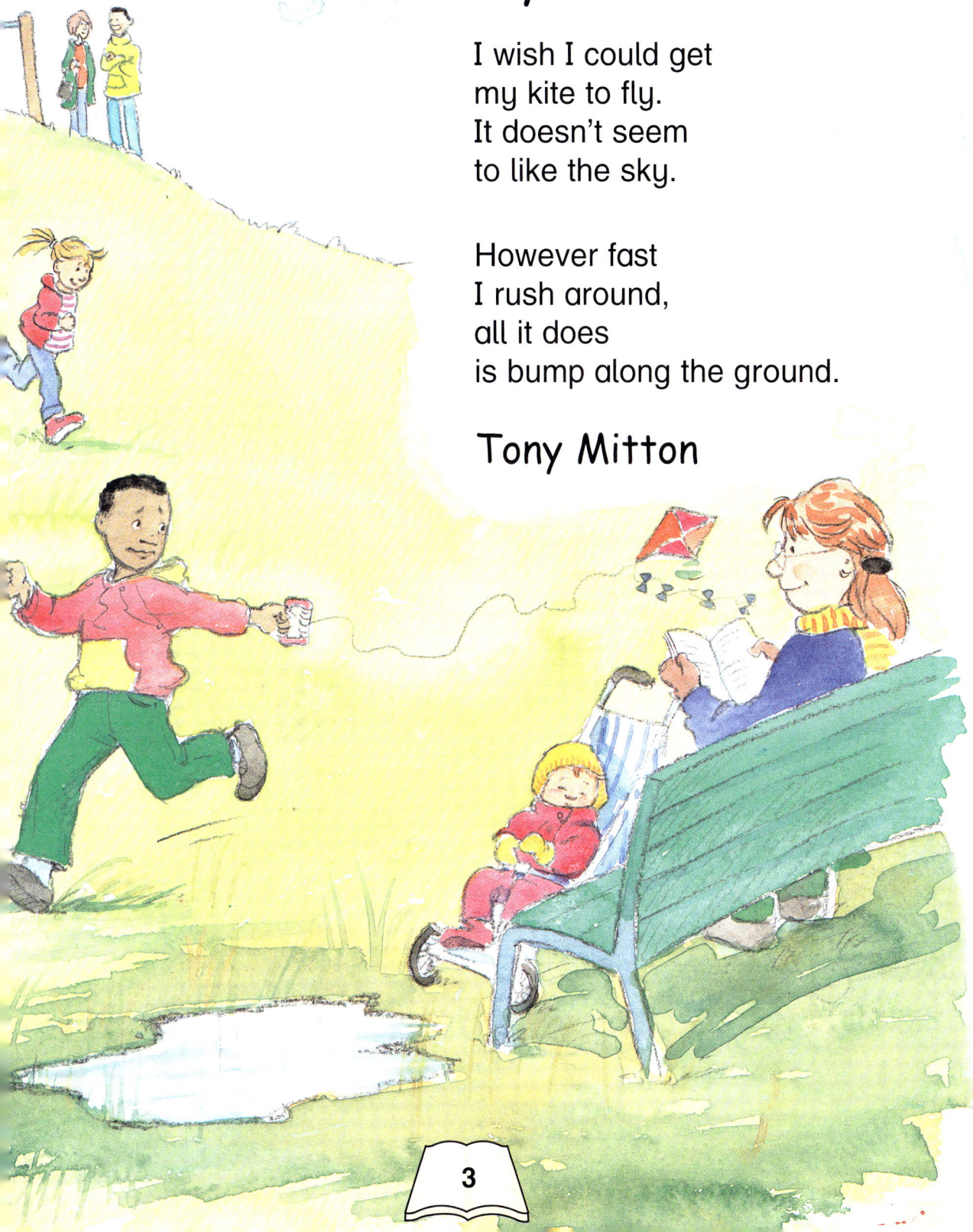

My Kite

I wish I could get
my kite to fly.
It doesn't seem
to like the sky.

However fast
I rush around,
all it does
is bump along the ground.

Tony Mitton

Snakes And Ladders

I played at Snakes and Ladders
with my little brother, Jake.
I went up the ladders
and he went down the snakes.
Then he went up some ladders
and it wasn't so much fun
when I went down the snakes
and my little brother won.

Marian Swinger

Baby's Toy

My little brother's nearly two
And really very bright,
And Mum and Dad bought lots of toys
They thought would be just right.

But do you know what he prefers
Whenever he's at play?
A saucepan and a tablespoon
To bang and bang all day.

Clive Webster

On the Playground

Children, children,
children jumping.
Children racing,
children bumping.
Children shouting,
children leaping,
children rolling,
children creeping.
Children crawling,
children dashing,
children falling,
children crashing.
Children, children,
children hopping.

There goes the bell.

Children, children,
children … stopping.

Wes Magee

In the Park

The smell of cut grass.

My friends are having a battle.

Laughing, shouting,
    chucking grass at each other.

I wish I hadn't argued with them.

Mike Jubb

Slinky Dog

Slinky dog is special,
He always makes me laugh.
His tail sticks up,
His tongue flops out,
His eyes are wide apart.

But best of all is his middle
– a shiny metal spring –
Which hops daft Slinky
Down the stairs
Ber-ding
  … ber-ding
    … ber-ding.

Patricia Leighton

Missing

Has anyone seen
    a furry old bear?
I've hunted here
And I've hunted there,
I've looked up high
And I've looked down low –
Under the bedclothes
Where he likes to go,
Inside the cupboards
Where he likes to hide,
In the back of the car
Where he likes to ride –
So, has anyone seen
    a furry old bear?
I still can't find him –
ANYWHERE!

Trevor Harvey

Boom Boom

"Who gave them a drum?"
Grumbles our Mum.

"It's driving me mad,"
Splutters our Dad.

"Can't we send the thing back?"
Complains Uncle Jack.

"Take their drumsticks away,"
Screams mean Auntie May.

"Oooh my ears, oooh my head,"
Groans Gran from her bed.

"I bought it, you know,"
Writes kind Auntie Flo.
(Who lives far away
In Borneo.)

Clare Bevan

Slide

At the top of the slide
I stop for a moment.
I want to pretend I'm a tree.
So I wave my arms
And gaze into the distance
To see what it is that trees see.
When I'm tired of that
And there's someone else waiting
It's
   down on my seat and

  w
     h
        e
           e
              e
                 e
                    !

Sue Cowling

Bouncy Castle

I spring,
I bounce
I touch the sky,

I watch
the birds
go flying by.

I glide,
I spin,
I skip the moon,

then dive
down to
a blue lagoon.

I ride
the surf,
I'm swimming free,

a dolphin
in the
crystal sea.

Then
jumping high,
wind in my face,

I shout
for joy,
I love this place.

To me
it's like
a birthday parcel.

Filled with fun
this
bouncy castle.

Tony Norman

It Isn't Raining on My Side of the Car

It isn't raining on my side of the car,
and I don't want to sit inside now we've travelled this far.
Please let me out, unlock the door,
there's a whole new beach for me to explore,
and it isn't raining on my side of the car.

On the side I'm on the sky is turning blue,
I can see a rainbow, the sun is shining through.
Let's go outside and start to play,
we've already wasted half the day,
and it isn't raining on my side of the car.

Brian Moses

Five Minutes More

Give us five minutes more, dad!
    Just five minutes more!
Time to fish in the rock pool
    and run along the shore.

Give us four minutes more, dad!
    We're not ready for tea!
We want to collect a few more shells
    And paddle a bit in the sea.

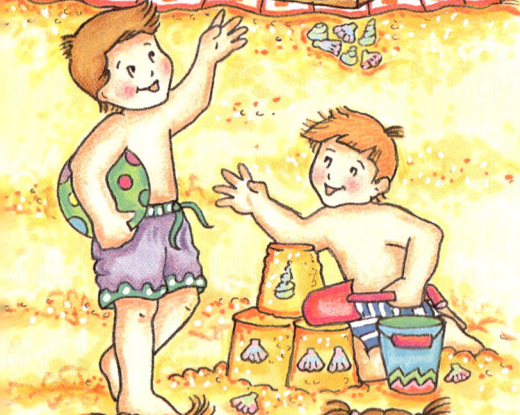

Give us three minutes more, dad!
    Time to jump through the waves!
Time to build a sandcastle,
    and make echoes in the caves.

Give us two minutes more, dad!
    Just one more go on the swings!
Just one more chase along the sands
    And then we'll gather our things.

We've had such a great day, dad!
    Picnicking and playing in the sun!
We never want it to end, dad,
    so just one more minute of fun?

    Please dad!

Moira Andrew

Beanie

Beanie is old,
And his walk is slow,
But we still play in the park,
Beanie,
Me and Mark.
In dog-years he's twenty-three or more,
So he must be a hundred and sixty-four!
But still we play in the park,
Beanie,
Me and Mark.
He can't catch his tail or the ball in mid-air,
And run as he did with the wind in his hair,
And he's long forgotten how to bark,
But still we play in the park,
Beanie,
Me and Mark.

Mary Green

Fair's Fair

I've got …
a train set, a Scalextric and a Playstation
but I never get to play on them.

Dad's always on them,
says he needs to know they work
so he can help me play with them properly.

That was ages ago now,
and he's still practising.
I never get to go on them.

What he doesn't know is that
his golf clubs make great swords and spears,
his old records and CDs are brilliant frisbees
and his guitar is a pretty good tennis racquet.

Fair's fair.

Paul Cookson

18

Midnight Feast Recipe

Ingredients

1 forgotten toothbrush
19 beanie bears
2 pairs of matching slippers
 (including fur and ears)
3 giant bottles of cola
6 packets of barbecue crisps
15 fun-size Mars Bars
1 bag of pic-n-mix
2 beds made up with duvets
1 joke without an end
9 and a half trips to the toilet
2 *very* best very-best-friends

Method

Mix well together, then
 transfer to the floor.
Set the alarm for midnight
 and close the bedroom door.

Danielle Sensier

Big Ted

Big Ted is fun to have around,
he's a really big-hearted bear.
I've loved him ever since the day
Dad won him at the fair.

If I bump Big Ted down the stairs
he never seems to worry,
he doesn't complain or make a fuss
or tell me I'll be sorry.

The smile upon his face
never seems to disappear.
He didn't even frown or wince
when Mum re-stitched his ear.

Big Ted worries about me
when I'm at school each day –
will I dress up warm enough
when I'm sent out to play?

He mothers me when mum's not there,
he understands when I'm sad,
he's never grumpy or sharp with me
and nothing makes him mad.

I'm almost as tall as him now,
but no matter how much I grow,
Big Ted is a special friend to me
and always will be, I know.

Brian Moses

Game Boy?

Grab that game Boy
Watch me go,
Whizz my hero
To and fro,
Beat those baddies,
Solve that maze,
Find and fight
For days and days,
Track that treasure,
Hit that score,
Splat those targets,
Zap some more,
Watch my thumbs
Until your minds whirl …
Look out, monsters,
Here comes GAME GIRL !!

Clare Bevan

Hopscotch

A hip hop hippity hop
yes it's time to play hopscotch
hip hop hippity hop
yes it's time to play hopscotch

a turn and a twist
we make a double fist
a jump and a spin
we go right in

a flop and a hop
I spin like a top
Jessie now stands upside down
her smile looks just like a frown

Hey!
a hip hop hippity hop
me and my friends play hopscotch

jumping
    laughing
       running
screaming
hip
    hop
       hippity
hop

we are all having fun
wanting to play
    till day is done
until Gloria the big bully
comes and yells

BOYS DON'T PLAY HOPSCOTCH!!!

Afua Cooper

Endings to Play With

Pages 2 and 3	bump	bumps	bumped	bumping
	jump	jumps	jumped	jumping
	rush	rushes	rushed	rushing
	stretch	stretches	stretched	stretching
Pages 6 and 7	crawling	crawl	crawls	crawled
	hopping	hop	hops	hopped

Pages 8 and 9	hunted	hunt	hunts	hunting
	likes	like	liked	liking
Pages 12 and 13	dive	dives	dived	diving
	skip	skips	skipped	skipping
	touch	touches	touched	touching
	watch	watches	watched	watching

Pages 16 and 17	collect	collects	collected	collecting
	paddle	paddles	paddled	paddling
Pages 18 and 19	practising	practise	practises	practised
Pages 20 and 21	complain	complains	complained	complaining
	grab	grabs	grabbed	grabbing
	solve	solves	solved	solving